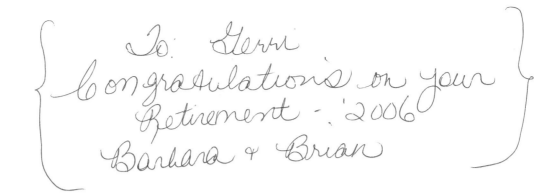

To: Gerri
Congratulations on your
Retirement - '2006
Barbara & Brian

WESTERN
NEWFOUNDLAND

AND GROS MORNE NATIONAL PARK

BRIAN BURSEY

with an introduction by MICHAEL BURZYNSKI

NIMBUS
PUBLISHING

Nimbus Publishing Limited
PO Box 9166
Halifax, NS   B3K 5M8
(902) 455-4286

Printed and bound in Singapore

Design: Kate Westphal, Graphic Detail Inc., Charlottetown, P.E.I.
Author photo: Marilyn Bursey

Library and Archives Canada Cataloguing in Publication
        Bursey, Brian C
        Western Newfoundland and Gros Morne National Park / photographs by
        Brian Bursey ; foreword by Michael Burzynski.

  ISBN 1-55109-572-6

1. Gros Morne National Park (N.L.)—Pictorial works. 2. Newfoundland and
Labrador—Pictorial works. I. Burzynski, Michael, 1954- II. Title.

FC2164.G76B86 2006   971.8   C2005-907806-5

We acknowledge the financial support of the Government of Canada through the Book Publishing Industry Development Program (BPIDP) and the Canada Council, and of the Province of Nova Scotia through the Department of Tourism, Culture and Heritage for our publishing activities.

Western Newfoundland

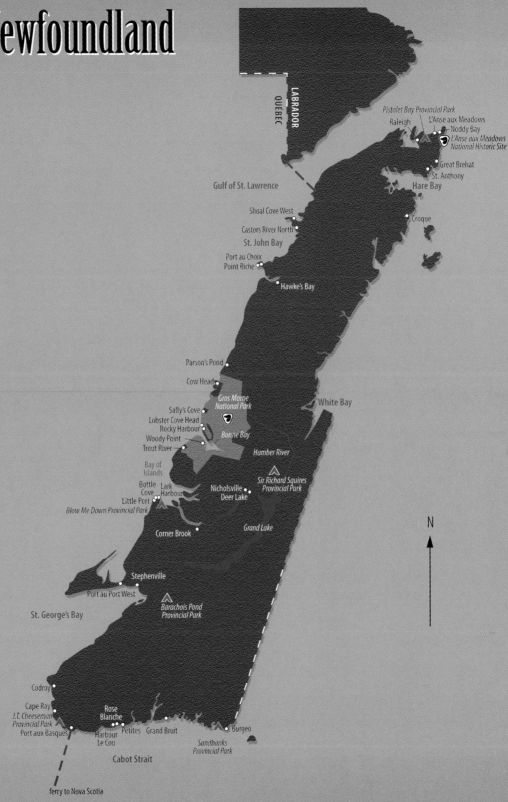

Legend

- ⬟ National Park
- ▲ Provincial Park
- ○ City/Town
- --- Ferry Service

QUEBEC
LABRADOR

Pistolet Bay Provincial Park
Raleigh
L'Anse aux Meadows
Noddy Bay
L'Anse aux Meadows National Historic Site
Great Brehat
St. Anthony
Hare Bay

Gulf of St. Lawrence

Shoal Cove West
Castors River North
St. John Bay
Croque

Port au Choix
Point Riche
Hawke's Bay

Parson's Pond

Cow Head

Gros Morne National Park
White Bay

Sally's Cove
Lobster Cove Head
Rocky Harbour
Bonne Bay
Woody Point
Trout River

Humber River

Bay of Islands
Sir Richard Squires Provincial Park

Bottle Cove
Lark Harbour
Nicholsville
Deer Lake
Little Port
Blow Me Down Provincial Park

Corner Brook
Grand Lake

N

Stephenville

Port au Port West

Barachois Pond Provincial Park

St. George's Bay

Codroy

Cape Ray
Rose Blanche
J.T. Cheeseman Provincial Park
Port aux Basques
Harbour Le Cou
Petites
Grand Bruit
Burgeo

Sandbanks Provincial Park

Cabot Strait

ferry to Nova Scotia

The Tablelands, Gros Morne National Park, overlook Bonne Bay and the community of Woody Point.

PREFACE

Geologically and geographically, western Newfoundland is a part of the Appalachian mountain chain of eastern North America. These mountains have been repeatedly glaciated, leaving dramatic cliffs and fiords throughout the region. Arable land is scarce, and largely limited to major river valleys.

Permanent settlement came late to western Newfoundland, with the population of the entire region numbering only a few hundred in the early nineteenth century. While development of the fishery and establishment of a newsprint mill in Corner Brook have greatly increased these numbers, moose and caribou continue to outnumber humans. This is not to say, however, that the region is lacking in human history. Successive waves of settlers—Aboriginal, Norse, Basque, French, English, Scottish, Irish—have all contributed to the unique flavour of the region.

Although the area is by no means northerly (Corner Brook is no further north than Paris or Vancouver), Newfoundland's location on the eastern edge of North America, and the cold sweep of the Labrador Current, bring long winters and harsh weather conditions, including the notoriously strong winds. Yet this is a land of stunning beauty. Summer and fall are characterized by long periods of fine weather and air of remarkable clarity. Colourful wildflowers abound, while dramatic mountains, sparkling rivers, abundant wildlife, and spectacular seascapes enchant the visitor at every turn. The changing landscapes of Gros Morne National Park, a UNESCO World Heritage Site, are typical of the scenic diversity of the region.

There is far more to western Newfoundland than can be captured by pictures. To fully experience this unique region, one must explore the trails of the Long Range Mountains, look for whales and icebergs near St. Anthony, and watch the sun set over the Gulf of St. Lawrence on a warm summer's evening with only the gulls and waves for companionship. It is hoped that this book will awaken fond memories for those who have already done these things, while inspiring the curiosity of those who have not yet visited.

Brian C. Bursey

Grand Bruit. This isolated fishing community on Newfoundland's southwest coast can only be reached by water.

INTRODUCTION: WIND

Foehn. Chinook. Typhoon. Santa Ana. Sirocco. Mistral. Haboob. Williwaw. Squamish. Suête. Throughout the world there are winds that control life, recurring winds that are predictable and violent enough to be granted a name—even a personality. It is a wind like these that rules the west coast of Newfoundland, shaping the lives of trees, animals, and humans. Strangely, in a province renowned for the poetry and quirkiness of its place names, this wind bears no name.

Wind brought life to this island. Repeated glaciations during the Ice Age had scraped Newfoundland bare. As the ice melted 12,500 years ago, it left a sterilized landscape of smooth rock, wet hollows, and vast boulder and gravel deposits. A few tiny islands of life may have survived along the coast, but most of the re-colonization of Newfoundland was done by immigrants, and most of those arrived in the arms of the wind: seeds and spores, insects, ballooning spiders, and birds drifted across the Gulf of St. Lawrence to this new found land.

To this day, strong winds are common in Newfoundland, especially along the west coast. Steady winds that blow off the ocean dry exposed tree buds and needles, pruning coastal trees into a dwarfed and flattened forest. This forest starts at the upper beach as a creeping groundcover, and then rises in a wedge shape inland, each tree taking shelter in the lee of another closer to the coast. Branches that stick up are nipped off by cold, dry winter winds, only those safe beneath the snow survive. The tops of trees are flagged: branches become ragged green tufts pointing downwind, all upwind branches die off. Branches become so tightly intertwined that they are impenetrable to hikers. You can walk over the top of these trees, or crawl along beneath them, but not push through them. Although the wind is anonymous, this elfin forest has a local name: Tuckamore. It is also found on the upper slopes of hills, at the treeline, and in sheltered hollows on the high plateaus.

The nameless wind sculpts the forest in another way. Some hills along the coast and at the foot of the mountains are swathed in low forest that seems to have been bulldozed in strips. Waves of green standing trees alternate up the hills with troughs filled with grey dead trunks and boughs. This forest is the result of strong winds rocking the tallest trees, damaging their roots, allowing fungi to invade, and causing the eventual death and collapse of infected trees. As new saplings grow in the clearings and the next row of taller trees topples over, each wave moves slowly downwind.

Wind and cool weather cause the treeline to ride low on the hills of the Long Range; in most places the forest rises to only two hundred metres above sea level. Because of this, the rounded hills wear a monk's tonsure of trees: ringed with green fuzz, they are bald on top and hunched on the landscape in meditative silence. Insects and wind control forests on the lowlands. Fire is a stranger here because the coastal influence ensures that summers are cool and damp. This encourages the growth of balsam fir (a tree that does not tolerate fire), and reduces the success of pines (which are now uncommon on the west coast of the Island). Although fires are rare, smoke is relatively common, drifting from burning forests in Labrador. During the day the smoky haze yellows the sky, but blazes to life again as the sun sets over Labrador.

Houses are squat and tight, clinging to the ground, surveying the skies with small dark windows. They are built to survive the wind. Place names such as Blow-Me-Down and Wreckhouse reflect the power of gusts, and truckers and other travellers are wise to heed the frequent wind warnings on radio. Houses have been torn apart, trains and trucks blown over, and boats lifted from their moorings by the nameless wind. In winter, sea ice can blow against the coast overnight, blocking it solidly and covering the ocean as far as the eye can see. Just as fast, wind from another direction can blow it all away. Vast fleets of drifting ice blocks can crush wharves and change beaches. Onshore winds are strong enough in some places to blow rocks up over the crests of cliffs, depositing them at the top of the cliff, instead of at the foot.

Wind blew explorers to these shores. First came the Maritime Archaic Indians, crossing from Labrador almost five thousand years ago. Palaeoeskimo peoples followed them two thousand years later as the climate got colder and the seals whelped farther south. Ancestors of the Beothuk also crossed the Strait of Belle Isle, and more recently, the Mi'kmaq came from Cape Breton. About a thousand years ago, the wind blew Viking longboats westward from Europe. These Norse explorers erected buildings at L'Anse aux Meadows and sailed the coast of Newfoundland, Labrador, and eastern North America. In the sixteenth century, Basque whalers used the same wind to hunt their giant prey along this coast, and then came waves of fishers and settlers.

Although this Island is isolated by water from the mainland, it is joined by wind. Vast air movements driven by the rotation of our planet push air from central North America eastward and northward. Pollution from the industrial centre of the continent moves across the Maritime provinces and out over Newfoundland. Even here, acidic precipitation and airborne pollutants are a concern. Even the wind can be misused.

There is a freshness to wind, a quickening as it blows against one's face and drives the taste of salt spray against one's lips. The stronger the wind, the more ravens, crows, and gulls seem to rejoice in flight, rising, diving, and somersaulting weightlessly along cliffs and above headlands. The rush of air is alive, carrying with it euphoria. Experience the wind that shapes the west coast of Newfoundland, let it buffet your ears, play with your hair, and rock you on your feet. Strain to hear its name.

Michael Burzynski

Fishing vessels at Rose Blanche. The name Rose Blanche is thought to be a corruption of the French "roche blanche", or white rock. There are numerous outcroppings of white granite in the area. Stone from nearby Petites was once quarried for use in the construction of the Court House in St. John's and in other public buildings throughout Newfoundland.

Facing page: *The Caribou*, entering Port aux Basques. Most visitors to western Newfoundland arrive via one of several large passenger/vehicle ferries connecting Newfoundland with North Sydney, Nova Scotia.

Catfish in Codroy. The fisheries continue to be the economic mainstay of many communities in western Newfoundland with shrimp, snow crab, cod and lobster being the most important species.

Facing page: These storage sheds in St. Lunaire show the ravages of wind and time.

This granite lighthouse located at Rose Blanche dates from 1873. It has been restored and is a popular tourist destination.

Facing page: Rose Blanche. Colourful houses, painted in traditional colours, are characteristic of communities along Newfoundland's southwest coast. Many of these colours were once used on fishing vessels, with "dory buff" and "boat bottom green" being perennial favourites.

A home-made anchor, or killick. Used to moor nets or small boats, killicks are made by enclosing a long stone in a flexible frame made from sticks or branches. This frame is bound at the top with twine and attached at the base to two heavier pieces of wood, known as killick claws.

Facing page: Codfish dry in the sun at Harbour Le Cou.

Trains no longer operate on the Island of Newfoundland, the passenger service having been terminated in 1969 with freight service following a few years later. Many communities continue to celebrate their historic links with this form of transportation, as evidenced by exhibits in Corner Brook (pictured here) and elsewhere.

Facing page: The Railway Heritage Centre, Port aux Basques.

Reflections at dawn, Petites. Bethany United Church was constructed in the late 1850s. It is thought to be the oldest wooden United, previously Methodist, church in North America.

Petites cannot be reached by road. This, combined with the fishery problems of recent years, resulted in a steady loss of population. By 2004, this once pros-perous community had been completely abandoned.

Facing page: A traditional fishing dory, Burgeo.

Twin Hills, north of Port aux Basques. These offshoots of the Long Range Mountains are unofficially referred to as the "Mae West Hills".

Facing page: Caribou are found throughout much of western Newfoundland. The Burgeo highway, Gros Morne National Park and the Hawke's Bay - St. Anthony region are particularly good viewing areas. Caribou start to grow their antlers in April and shed them in late fall.

Above and facing page: Early summer brings a profusion of flora to western Newfoundland. Fireweed, rhodora and bunchberry flowers (above) are especially common.

At left: The Atlantic puffin is the provincial bird of Newfoundland and Labrador. Since puffins nest in burrows dug into soft turf, they are vulnerable to a variety of predators. Nesting on islands and coastal cliffs helps reduce this threat.

The pitcher plant, floral emblem of
Newfoundland and Labrador. This unusual
plant is named for its pitcher-like leaves.
Insects, attracted by nectar, are trapped
inside by downward pointing hairs,
where they eventually drown in the pool
of rainwater which collects there.
Nutrients from their bodies are absorbed
by the plant.

Facing page: Rhodora, a flowering shrub,
blooms in early June.

Above: Eroded limestone formations, Port au Port.

At left: Gypsum occurs at several locations in the Bay St. George area, and has been mined for wallboard production at Flat Bay. This occurrence is at Romaines Brook, near Stephenville.

Facing page: Beluga in Codroy Harbour. These gregarious whales are occasional visitors to Newfoundland waters.

Above: Fall colours.

At left: Our Lady of Mercy Church, Port au Port West, is the largest wooden church on the island of Newfoundland.

Facing page: Bottle Cove, an abandoned fishing settlement at the southwest entrance to the Bay of Islands.

Coastline near Lark Harbour.

Facing page: Fishing vessels, Little Port Harmon, Stephenville.

Fall colours.

Facing page: A root cellar in Norris Point.

Yard art, Lark Harbour.

Facing page: Buttercups surround an aging pick-up truck in the fishing/farming community of Robinsons.

An Atlantic salmon jumps Big Falls on the Humber River. Sir Richard Squires Memorial Park, the first provincial park in Newfoundland and Labrador, was established here in 1954.

Facing page: These colourful fishing vessels at Frenchman's Cove, Bay of Islands, are used primarily in the lobster fishery.

This hydroelectric station was built to supply power to the pulp and paper complex at Corner Brook.

Below: Bridge over the Humber River at Nicholsville.

Facing page: Corner Brook, as seen from Cook's Lookout. From 1763 to 1767, Captain James Cook surveyed a large part of the coast of Newfoundland, producing the first large scale hydrographic charts of the area. After his success in Newfoundland, he was chosen to carry out exploration and mapping in the southern Pacific a few years later.

Everyday sights in autumn are spectacular.

Facing page: Margaret Bowater Park, Corner Brook. Fall colours brighten the banks of Corner Brook Stream.

The Insectarium, with its live butterfly pavilion, is a popular tourist stop in Deer Lake.

Facing page: An abundance of rivers and the Atlantic salmon's reputation as a superb game fish have made western Newfoundland a mecca for sport fishers since the 1800s. The Humber River (pictured) is noted for its large fish, with salmon being caught in excess of thirty pounds.

Green Gardens, situated in the south-western corner of Gros Morne National Park, rewards hikers with spectacular coastal scenery, including sea stacks and sea caves.

The Tablelands owe their distinct colouration to peridotite, a greenish black rock that weathers a rusty brown. Formed deep within the earth, peridotite was forced to the surface in western Newfoundland through the collision of the vast continental plates that make up the earth's crust. This unusual exposure was a prime reason for the designation of the Gros Morne area as a World Heritage Site by UNESCO.

The red fox occurs in a variety of colours, including yellow, brown, black and silver.

Facing page: The road to Trout River. Because peridotite is toxic to most forms of vegetation, little grows in the Tablelands, in marked contrast to the well wooded hillsides which mark the boundaries of the area. Those plants which do survive often take on unusual forms. A foot-high spruce tree can be centuries old.

More than twenty members of the orchid family occur in western Newfoundland. The showy lady's slipper, shown here, blooms in early July.

Facing page: The lighthouse at Woody Point.

Native to Labrador, moose were intro-
duced to the island of Newfoundland
in 1878 and again in 1904. The moose
population in western Newfoundland
currently approximates the number of
human residents. Moose/vehicle collisions
are common, particularly after dusk and
in the early morning, often with disas-
trous consequences for both humans and
animals.

Facing page: The snowshoe hare was intro-
duced to the island of Newfoundland from
Nova Scotia during the 1800s to provide
an additional food source for outport
residents. Locally, but incorrectly, referred
to as "rabbits", these hares change their
colour with the seasons, becoming almost
entirely white by late fall.

The figurehead—*Europa*.

Facing page: the *Europa*, a steel bark constructed in 1911, is one of the more unusual "cruise ships" offering tours of western Newfoundland.

Waterfalls on Bakers Brook, Gros Morne National Park.

Facing page: The lighthouse at Lobster Cove Head, constructed in 1897, is open to the public as a tourist attraction. The covered walkway between the light tower and lightkeeper's residence provided protection from the elements.

Fishing vessels, Rocky Harbour.

Facing page: Waves wash over multi-coloured boulders at Lobster Cove, Gros Morne National Park.

Western Newfoundland has remarkable sunsets, a theme reflected in the artwork adorning the bow of this fishing vessel.

Sand drifts inland near Western Brook, smothering the coastal forest with dunes that can exceed 30 metres in height.

Facing page: Beach at Shallow Bay, Gros Morne National Park.

The Whale Cave, or "Big Oven", near Raleigh is one of the largest sea caves in the world. The cave is 20 metres wide at the entrance and extends inward for a distance of 100 metres.

Facing page: Black bears are agile climbers. Omnivores, their diet ranges from berries to moose.

Hand-operated wooden winches, like these located in the community of Mainland on the Port au Port Peninsula, are still used to haul small fishing vessels ashore. The Port au Port area is the centre of French language and culture in New-foundland and Labrador.

Facing page: Buttercups surround an abandoned fishing boat in Noddy Bay.

In late June and July, capelin roll onto beaches to spawn, their eggs adhering to sand and gravel until hatching about fifteen or twenty days later. The small fish are commercially harvested, and are an important food source for a variety of species such as cod, seals and whales.

Facing page: Fishing stages line the shoreline at Parson's Pond.

Seal skins cure on outdoor racks in Shoal Cove East. Sealing is an important seasonal activity for fishermen along northern coasts of Newfoundland.

Facing page: Lobster fishing gear at Sally's Cove. Early residents of western Newfoundland found lobster so plentiful that it was collected for bait in the cod fishery. By the early 1900s, however, most of the lobster harvested was finding its way into small local canneries. The fishermen were typically paid $0.90 to $1.00 per 100 lobsters, regardless of size!

Blue Flag Iris

Facing page: Gros Morne Mountain, at 806 metres (2644 feet), is the second highest on the Island of Newfoundland.

The trail to Western Brook Pond leads visitors past several small ponds, across peat bogs, and through mixed growth boreal forest. There is an abundance of wildflowers, including blue flag iris, twin-flower (facing page), arethusa or dragon's mouth orchid (left), indian pipe (below), and marsh marigolds.

This statue in St. Anthony commemorates Sir Wilfred Grenfell, a medical missionary who first came to Newfoundland in 1892. Grenfell was appalled by the lack of medical services in northern Newfoundland and along the Labrador coast and dedicated the remainder of his life to improving the conditions there. Ultimately, his skills as a writer and fund raiser would enable him to construct a series of hospitals, nursing stations and orphanages in Labrador, northern Newfoundland, and along the Quebec north shore.

Facing page: The Arches, a provincially maintained public beach, is located just outside the northern boundary of Gros Morne National Park. The site features a series of unusual wave-carved limestone formations.

At left: Western Brook Pond, as viewed from its eastern end. The cliffs surrounding this glacially carved lake are more than 600 metres high.

Facing page: Many early Newfoundland settlers came from southern England, which has relatively few lakes. The result was that they named almost every area of fresh water, regardless of size, after the small ponds with which they were familiar.

Western Brook Pond is just one, albeit the best known, of several glacially carved finger lakes in Gros Morne National Park. While these lakes were once true fiords, a rebounding of the sea bed following the last period of glaciation left these bodies of water well inland from the Gulf of St. Lawrence.

Playful humpback whales are found throughout the waters of western Newfoundland during the summer months. Named for their unusually shaped dorsal fins, humpbacks are five metres long and weigh two tonnes at birth. Adults can reach 12 metres in length and weigh 40 tonnes, while the characteristically white flippers can exceed four metres.

Facing page: The dogberry, or mountain ash, provides a welcome food source for robins and other birds during the winter months.

Costumed re-enactors bring the Viking age to life at Norstead, a replica port of trade.

Facing page: The 1000 year old camp at L'Anse aux Meadows is the only authenticated Norse site in the New World. The location is a National Historic Site and has been designated as a World Heritage Site by UNESCO.

Snow crab, St. Lunaire

Facing page: Clouds move in across the coastal lowlands of the Northern Peninsula on a stormy fall day. The coastal plain extending northward from Rocky Harbour was once below sea level.

Overleaf: Although the glaciers of east Greenland and the Canadian Arctic contribute a few of the icebergs seen in Newfoundland waters, most originate from west Greenland. Here, fingers of the 3,000 metre thick Greenland icecap reach the sea, where large sections break off through a process known as calving.